BARRY SANDERS

LION WITH A QUIET ROAR

By Howard Reiser

CHILDRENS PRESS ®
CHICAGO

Photo Credits

Cover, Focus on Sports; 6, ©Al Messerschmidt/Focus on Sports;
8, UPI/Bettmann; 9, Reuters/Bettmann; 11, 13, Focus on Sports; 14, *The
Wichita Eagle*; 17, ©Patrick Murphy-Racey/Focus on Sports; 19, AP/Wide
World; 20, ©Antonio Hansen; 21, 23, AP/Wide World; 24, Reuters/
Bettmann; 27, AP/Wide World; 28, UPI/Bettmann; 31, AP/Wide World;
33, 34, ©Louis A. Raynor/Sports Chrome East/West; 36, 37, 38, AP/Wide
World; 39, Reuters/Bettmann; 41, 42, Focus on Sports; 44, AP/Wide World;
47, UPI/Bettmann

Project Editor: Shari Joffe
Design: Beth Herman Design Associates
Photo Research: Jan Izzo

Acknowledgments

The author would like to thank Robert McG. Thomas, Jr., of the
New York Times; Mike Murray of Media Relations of the Detroit Lions;
Peter Hayes, editor of *College and Pro Football News Weekly*; and the
Public Relations Department of the National Football League.

Reiser, Howard.
    Barry Sanders : (lion with a quiet roar) / by Howard Reiser.
        p. cm–(Sports stars)
    Summary: A brief biography of running back Barry Sanders,
    the all-time leading ball-carrier of the Detroit Lions.
    ISBN 0-516-04377-3
    1. Sanders, Barry, 1968- –Juvenile literature. 2. Football
    players–United States–Biography–Juvenile literature. [1. Sanders,
    Barry, 1968- . 2. Football players.] I. Title. II. Series.
    GV939.S18R45   1993
    796.332'092–dc20   93-19780
    [B]   CIP
                                                    AC

BARRY SANDERS

LION WITH A QUIET ROAR

Many people consider Barry Sanders the best running back in professional football. Barry appreciates the compliments. But he does not feel he deserves special praise.

"I am just like any other person," says Barry, the all-time leading ball carrier for the NFL Detroit Lions. "I still feel uncomfortable when fans approach me, and make a big fuss. I am merely a human being, not a god."

Sanders has been a football hero since winning the Heisman Trophy in 1988. That award is given annually to the best college football player in America. Yet Barry has always remained humble, shy, soft-spoken, and respectful of others.

Barry avoids a tackle on the way to scoring a touchdown.

"Barry Sanders is the best running back I have ever seen," says Lions head coach Wayne Fontes. "But he is more than that. Barry is a wonderful person. That is what makes him so special."

Barry sails over the top for a touchdown.

———————— ★ ★ ★ ————————

While many stars love attention, Barry prefers to praise his teammates. Barry knows he is a great running back. But he also knows that he could not do as well as he does without the help of his offensive linemen. They block the players on the other team when Barry or the other Lion running backs have the ball.

Barry has shown his gratitude by giving gifts to his teammates after the football season is over. "I simply wish to express my appreciation to my teammates," says Barry, when asked about the gifts.

Barry's attitude stems from his experience as a high-school football player. Even though he was a talented player, he was not given the chance to play as a starter until his senior year in high school.

Barry with some of his teammates

"Because of my own personal experiences, I learned to have greater respect, and understanding, for others," Barry says. "I learned that a second-string player, or one who is not in the limelight, deserves as much respect as a popular starter. Everyone contributes to a team's success."

Barry's outstanding character has helped make him one of the most popular athletes in America. "He is simply great, both as a player and as a person," says Peter Hayes, editor of *College and Pro Football News Weekly*. "He's polite, modest, and gives to charity. Barry is a great role model."

In high school, Barry played basketball and football.

The holder of thirteen all-time Detroit Lions records, Barry was born on July 16, 1968, in Wichita, Kansas. He was the seventh of eleven children born to William and Shirley Sanders. Barry and his family lived in a three-bedroom home.

As a boy, Barry helped out with his father's roofing business. He often carried hundreds of pounds of asphalt on his back. The work was hard. But it helped teach Barry discipline. "My dad was tougher on me than any football coach I ever had," Barry recalls.

Growing up, Barry loved sports. In fact, he liked basketball better than football. But his father believed that Barry would have a better chance of getting a college football scholarship than a basketball scholarship. So Mr. Sanders encouraged Barry to concentrate on football.

At North High School in Wichita, Barry played on the football team. However, it was not until the fourth game of his senior year that Barry was given the opportunity to play regularly at tailback. This was the same position his older brother, Byron, had played at Wichita North.

Once given the chance, Barry proved to be an exciting runner. He showed speed and tricky moves. Despite his late start, Barry gained 1,417 rushing yards during the season. There was no question that he was an outstanding talent. But he was only 5 feet 8 inches tall, and weighed merely 170 pounds. Many big-time college coaches considered him too small for their football programs.

Barry has always been an exciting runner.

"He's a tremendous talent," agreed University of Oklahoma coach Barry Switzer. But Switzer was not impressed enough. "Barry was too small," Switzer later explained. Another coach answered sarcastically when asked about Sanders. "We do not need another midget," said the coach.

Those coaches who were not interested in having Barry on their teams later learned to regret it. Oklahoma State University signed Barry to a football scholarship in time for the 1986 season.

"We have a real big winner here," exclaimed assistant coach George Walstad, after signing Barry. Head coach Pat Jones soon agreed with Walstad. "Barry is short, but he is very strong and fast," said Jones. "It is almost impossible for one person to tackle him."

During Barry's first two years at Oklahoma State, it would have been impossible for an

Barry with Oklahoma State head coach Pat Jones

entire team to tackle him. That's because Barry spent most of the time sitting on the bench, as a backup to the great Thurman Thomas. Thurman went on to star with the NFL Buffalo Bills.

Barry would have liked to have seen more action. But he understood that he had to be patient. He knew that he would eventually be given the chance to succeed Thomas as Oklahoma State's star running back.

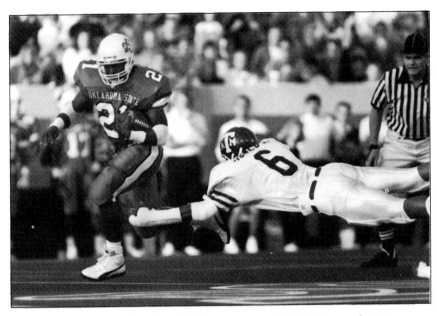
Barry slips by a defender during a game at Oklahoma State.

He finally received his opportunity in 1988, in his junior year. And Barry made the most of it. His exciting running skills thrilled the nation, while frustrating Oklahoma State's opponents. He led his team to a record of 10 and 2, and by the end of the season, had broken or tied 24 National Collegiate Athletic Association records. These included gaining more rushing yards (2,628) and scoring more touchdowns (39) in a single season than any college player in history.

--- ★ ★ ★ ---

In recognition of his achievements, Barry won the prestigious Heisman Trophy, awarded annually to the nation's best college football player. Although most people had expected Barry to win the Heisman, Barry had not given much thought to receiving the honor. "I do not feel comfortable talking about myself," said Barry toward the end of the 1988 season. "It makes it appear as though I am bragging. I have great respect for the Heisman Trophy. But winning the Heisman is not my goal. It is not one of my priorities."

Still, Barry was very proud when he won the award. Not surprisingly, however, he used the occasion to praise his teammates. "I certainly had a lot of help," he said, after winning the trophy. "As far as the team is concerned, it is something everyone can be proud of."

Barry won the Heisman Trophy in 1988.

Barry scores another touchdown for OSU.

A few weeks later, when Barry led his team to a 62-14 trouncing of Wyoming in the Holiday Bowl, his unselfishness was once again evident. In only three quarters of play, Barry rushed for 222 yards and scored five touchdowns. He needed just four more yards to break the Holiday Bowl record set by Southern Methodist's Craig James in 1980. But Barry chose to sit out the rest of the game to let others play. This cost him the chance to break the record.

"The record was not important to me," said Barry after the game. "The important thing was that we won." Coach Jones was not surprised by Barry's actions. "It shows you the great person he is," said Jones.

★ ★ ★

A person must work hard to achieve success. Knowing this, Barry spent many, many hours lifting weights and practicing on the college football field. "I never saw anyone work as hard as Barry," remarked Dallas Cowboys strength coach Jerry Schmidt. Said Barry's mother, Shirley, "Barry has always worked hard, just like his father."

Barry was faced with a tough decision in the spring of 1989: whether to return to Oklahoma State for his senior year, or leave college so that he could become eligible for the 1989 NFL draft. The idea of immediately turning professional was very tempting. Because Barry was such a great player, he would be offered a lot of money to play in the NFL. He knew that the money would be a great help to his family.

Talking with the press during a break in a team workout

Barry loosens up during a Detroit Lions mini-camp.

Barry's father wanted his son to become a professional. He worried that if Barry returned to college, he might hurt himself playing football in his senior year. Mr. Sanders warned Barry that if this were to happen, the NFL might not be as interested in him the next season.

Barry did not make a hasty decision. He mulled over all the questions in his mind. Finally, he chose to follow his father's advice and become a professional.

Barry was selected in the first round of the 1989 NFL draft by the Detroit Lions. He was the third player to be picked overall. On September 7, 1989, he smiled broadly as he signed a five-year, $9.5 million contract with the Lions. This made Barry the highest-paid rookie in history.

Right after he signed the contract, Barry again showed his concern for others. He donated $250,000 to the Paradise Baptist Church in Wichita. His mother had been a founder of the church thirty-six years before. When asked about the donation, Barry said smilingly, "I'm just spreading the wealth around."

The Lion coaches weren't at all worried about Barry's size. They had seen him run the 40-yard dash in 4.3 seconds, bench press 225 pounds 16 times, and jump an incredible $41\frac{1}{2}$ inches into the air.

Now weighing a muscular 203 pounds, Barry had a great season in 1989. He gained 1,470 yards, breaking the Lions single-season and rookie records held by Billy Sims. He also finished only ten yards behind the league's leading rusher for the season, Christian Okoye of the Kansas City Chiefs.

It's not easy to bring Barry down when he has the ball.

Had he wanted to, Barry easily could have won the rushing title that year. In the last game of the season, against the Atlanta Falcons, Sanders scored three touchdowns. So in the fourth quarter, with the Lions ahead, Coach Fontes gave Sanders a rest. Then he realized that Barry needed only ten more yards to become the NFL's leading rusher. Just one or two more carries would do it. "Do you want to go in?" he asked Barry. "Coach," Barry answered, "give the ball to Tony [Paige]. Let's just win it and go home." Barry didn't care about winning the rushing title. He cared only about his team winning the game. Later, he explained, "When everyone is out for statistics—you know, individual fulfillment—that's when trouble starts. I don't want to ever fall victim to that."

Ready for action during a Pro Bowl game

———————————— ★ ★ ★ ————————————

Paige entered the game. This prevented Barry from finishing first in rushing. But it did not prevent him from winning the NFC Rookie of the Year award, and being chosen to start in the Pro Bowl game.

Barry followed up his great rookie season with another outstanding year in 1990. This time, he did win the league rushing title, with 1,304 yards. He was the first Lion to earn the honor since Byron "Whizzer" White did it in 1940. White, by the way, went on to become a United States Supreme Court justice, serving for thirty-one years before retiring in 1993.

Voted in 1990 to be a Pro-Bowl starter for the second straight year, Barry was now largely recognized as football's best running back. "He has great moves," said Fontes. "He will run into tacklers and, suddenly, you will see Barry come out of the line. O.J. Simpson was like that."

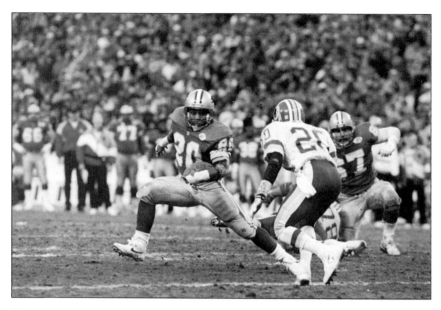

Says one player of Barry, "He's in a class by himself, he's so quick."

Simpson, a retired Hall of Famer, also marveled at Barry's talent. "Usually, a runner may make one or two real good moves during a 20–yard run," Simpson said. "Not Barry. He could do it five times."

Barry is not one to call attention to himself. Yet he admits, "I often find it exciting to watch game films and see some of my moves. I improvise as I go along."

Barry leaves a defender in the dust.

★ ★ ★

Barry continued his brilliant play in 1991 and 1992, making the Pro Bowl for his third and fourth straight years. In 1991, he led the league in rushing touchdowns, with 17, and helped spark the Lions to a 12 and 4 record, the first winning season of Barry's pro career. And his 1,548 rushing yards were only 15 yards fewer than Dallas Cowboy Emmitt Smith's league-leading 1,563. "He's in a class by himself," says Smith. "He's so quick."

Barry fends off two opponents while hanging onto the ball.

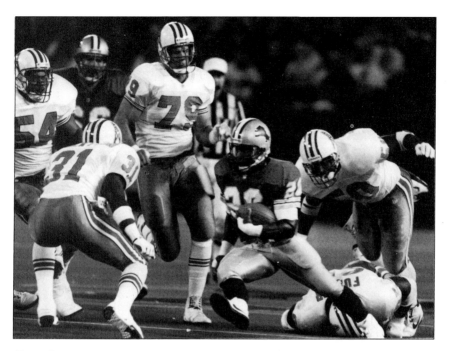

Barry's strength and speed make up for his lack of height.

From 1991 to 1993, Barry finished behind Emmitt Smith for the NFC rushing title. But in 1994, Barry came back with a superb season. He collected 1,883 yards—easily the best rushing total in the NFL. In one game, he rushed for an incredible 237 yards! Teammate Herman Moore marveled at Barry's newfound power, saying, "It's like he doesn't want to be tackled...ever!"

Those who have known Barry a long time are thrilled to celebrate his accomplishments. Says Lions nose tackle Jerry Ball, "Barry's got character and he's got commitment. He sets a wonderful example for everyone." Adds Fontes, "Barry Sanders has always provided an inspiration. It could be on the field, on the airplane, anywhere. He simply makes everyone feel much better."

Barry is proud of his success. Still, he is disappointed that the Lions have had only one winning season since he joined the team in 1989. "It's frustrating when you are not winning," admits Barry. "But you must always continue to play hard. You must never give up. You must always have faith."

Barry believes that the Lions can become one of the league's best teams in the near future. "I want to wear at least one championship ring," he says.

A quiet moment in the locker room

No one knows whether Barry Sanders will achieve that goal. But one thing is certain: he will always continue to respect others, whether they are rich or poor, strong or weak. "Everyone should be treated with dignity," Barry says. "To me, it does not matter how much money a person earns, or the type of work he does. I judge someone on his or her merits, on his or her character. That's the important thing."

When Barry goes back home to Wichita, he's just another
member of the family.

★ ★ ★

Barry owns a home outside Pontiac, Michigan. During the off-season, he often visits his family and friends in Wichita, Kansas. "It's always great to go back and see everyone," says Barry.

Barry hopes to play football for many years to come. Understandably, he has not given serious thought to what he will do after he retires from football. But more likely than not, it will involve helping people—helping make their lives more meaningful and enjoyable. To Barry Sanders, this is even more important than making his exciting moves during a 20-yard run.

Chronology

1968 – Barry Sanders, the seventh of eleven children of William and Shirley Sanders, is born in Wichita, Kansas, on July 16.

1985 – As a senior, Barry begins playing tailback for the North High School football team. He has a great season, gaining 1,417 rushing yards.

1986 – Barry receives a scholarship to play football at Oklahoma State University. For two years, he serves as a backup for running back Thurman Thomas.

1988 – Barry sparks his team to a record of 10 wins and 2 losses, and breaks or ties 24 National Collegiate Athletic Association records.
   – Barry wins the Heisman Trophy, awarded annually to best college football player in America.

1989 – Barry leaves Oklahoma State in his senior year to enter the NFL draft. Picked in the first round and third in the draft overall, he signs a five-year contract with the Detroit Lions. He immediately donates $250,000 of his contract money to the Paradise Baptist Church in Wichita.
   – Barry establishes a Lions single-season and rookie record by gaining 1,470 yards. He is also voted NFC Rookie of the Year, and is selected to start in the NFL Pro Bowl.

1990-91 – Barry gains 1,304 yards on the ground and wins his second straight NFL rushing title.

1991-92 – Barry leads the NFL with 17 touchdowns and finishes second in rushing with 1,548 yards. He is named NFC Player of the Year by the Pro Football Writers' Association and *Football Magazine*.

1992-93 – Barry becomes the first player in history to gain more than 1,500 total yards in rushing and receiving in each of his first four years in the NFL. He also becomes the Lions' all-time leading rusher, with 5,674 yards.

1993-94 – Barry rushes for 1,115 yards and leads Detroit to a 10-6 record and the NFC Central title. He is named to the Pro Bowl for the fifth straight year.

1994-95 – Barry reclaims the NFL rushing title with 1,883 yards. He is named the 1994 Sportsman of the Year by *The Sporting News*. The season ends badly, however, as Barry is held to a career-worst –1 yard in a playoff loss to the Green Bay Packers.

About the Author

Howard Reiser has been a well-known New York City newspaper reporter, columnist, and bureau chief. He has also worked as a labor news writer and editor. Today a political speechwriter, Mr. Reiser covered the major news stories in New York City for more than twenty-five years.

Mr. Reiser has written several other books for the *Sports Stars* series, including *Nolan Ryan, Scottie Pippen,* and *Jim Abbott.* He and his wife, Adrienne, live in New York. They have four children: Philip, Helene, Steven, and Stuart.